My
Soul
Lives On

My
Soul
Lives On

BRENDAN BARRY

iUniverse LLC
Bloomington

MY SOUL LIVES ON

iUniverse books may be ordered through booksellers or by contacting:

iUniverse LLC
1663 Liberty Drive
Bloomington, IN 47403
www.iuniverse.com
1-800-Authors (1-800-288-4677)

ISBN: 978-1-4917-1994-7 (sc)
ISBN: 978-1-4917-1993-0 (e)

Printed in the United States of America.

iUniverse rev. date: 02/18/2014

Contents

Foreword

On Friday, June 1st, 2007, Brendan recited an Irish poem during the long-awaited wedding ceremony of Brendan's father Tim and soon-to-be stepmom, Leighanne. While Leighanne and Brendan danced, she teased her new stepson. "I bet you never thought your stepmom could dance like this." Brendan answered her back, saying, "You're not my stepmom, you're my mom." After a childhood punctuated with rejection by his biological mother, Brendan's greatest wish—to have a mom in his life—was finally realized.

The night after the wedding, Brendan attended a party at a friend's house where there was the usual cache of beer, pot and cocaine. Brendan made the choice to go on a beer run with his friends to a store just two miles down the road. On the return trip, the driver lost control at over 90 MPH, causing the vehicle to leave the road and flip multiple times. Brendan's brain stem had snapped, leaving him brain dead. The driver and backseat passenger survived.

What appears to be a straightforward story of family connection and subsequent tragedy, however, is anything but. The true story of Brendan Barry lies in his struggle with learning difficulties, among them ADHD, ODD, depression, adjustment disorder, continuous attempts to overcome rejection from a biological mother with her own emotional baggage, his own rejection of clinical treatment in favor of self-medication, court ordered rehab, and a host of other organic and social problems that found a creative outlet in, among other things, cooking, music, and poetry.

Like most LD kids, Brendan was more than smart—he had a considerably high IQ that emphasized the dichotomy between intelligence and classroom achievement. People who knew him best describe him as affable, energetic, uncommonly engaging, bright, genuine, entertaining, confident without a trace of arrogance, and a truly creative thinker. He was wise beyond his years and simultaneously naïve about the repercussions of his impulsive behaviors.

In many ways, Brendan was the poster child for why treatment for learning disabilities more often fails. In a rare, uncensored piece he wrote about himself, he described what it was like to be in his skin.

Brendan's Inside Look

This is the inside look about me, Brendan Barry. I'm a white suburban kid who lives my life thinking I'm untouchable. I live my life like a superhero. I always involve myself in something that could get me caught, but somehow always escape. But like every hero, your last days of being unknown don't last forever. When that day comes, your life will be under the microscope.

My troubles didn't really start till I was 13, in the 8th grade. So I'll briefly fill in the gap from birth till then. I was told from the beginning I have always been in trouble of some sort. Whether it was digging through cupboards, walking in mall water fountains, or in kindergarten convincing classmates they were gonna die of lead poisoning. These same behaviors lasted through elementary and middle school and progressively got worse once I reached 8th grade. I was 13 starting at a new school, Churchville.

I forgot to say I have severe ADHD. No need to worry cause the medical field has many fixes. One of the popular ones is Ritalin aka Speed for Retards. Their theory is the stimulant has an opposite effect for ADHD kids. They're right. That shit fucked me up, but not in an enjoyable way. I hated it. I would sit in a classroom with my mouth shut and my brain in a daze. I'm an outgoing, energetic kid. That shit ain't for me. So I started spitting it out! Right? Not me.

Tim, Brendan's father, wrote in the eulogy of his son about the challenges and joys of watching Brendan grow up, both in spite of and because of his differences.

From his birth at 10 lbs., through his toddler years, Brendan never ceased to amaze me, not only with his inquisitive desire to learn, but his determination to try harder. He ran before he could walk. At age three, he had mastered swimming under water and riding a two-wheeler, both unassisted. He was not your typical little boy. While growing up in our neighborhood, he may have been the youngest by a couple of years, but he could hold the interest of the other children by capturing bugs, fishing, climbing trees and outrunning his older sister. Brendan loved to visit the neighbors, especially the ones that baked, and returned home with treats for him and his sister. After seeing a number of home gardens, Brendan asked me to start a tomato garden where he took great pride in showing off, especially to his grandparents who were avid gardeners. Brendan loved playing catch and golf in the backyard; he loved the alone time as little boys with their fathers often do.

As Brendan progressed through elementary school, he was different than most, always a little more active and somewhat smarter than his peers. After having him tested, our suspicions were correct. Brendan's IQ was in the superior range.

Brendan showed a passion for music. He started playing the drums in the school band and his interest in music only increased as he got older. Some of his other achievements included:

- *Math Master Championship Award Grade 4*
- *Member of the Rochester Recreation Swim Team*
- *Member of the Chili Youth Lacrosse Team*
- *Member of the Gates-Chili Youth Basketball League*
- *Recognized by the New York's Young Poets 1998*
- *Member of the Mount Morris JHS Basketball Team*

Brendan loved the outdoors, he loved camping trips, exploring, fishing on the river or some backwoods stream, and sharing what he had found. During these outings one thing remained constant: a new friend was made along the way.

At the tender age of thirteen, without regard for his own wellbeing, Brendan jumped into a rain-swollen creek to save the life of his best friend Aubrey, a gift to the L family that will always be remembered.

While attending JHS, Brendan demonstrated the ability to solve complex algebraic equations in his head, though he had yet to take an algebra class. He became a member of the Chili Fire Department Explorer Post. Outside of school, Brendan's passions were animals, his love of dogs second to none, his involvement in animal rescues showing his unselfish compassion. When life's troubles or current events started to affect Brendan, he would turn to paper and pen.

Brendan's sister, Caitlin, spoke of similar qualities at his funeral, chief among them the lessons she had learned from his examples of adaptation, acceptance, and generosity.

If you were to ask why I am who I am today, the response would be simple: Brendan. Looking back as far as I can remember, my universe has centered around one person, and I could never be more proud of someone's presence on this planet. As far back as I can remember, no matter what the situation was, Brendan was the biggest part of my life. We had an amazing bond that let us rely on each other all throughout the years.

It may sound cliché, but Brendan taught me more valuable life lessons that anyone I have ever encountered. He taught me to never pass judgments. It's easy to assume things about people that we do not know. His entire life he has been making friends with the people that no one else takes the time to speak with. He has friends from every walk of life, from the overweight outcast in school to the bums on Monroe Avenue.

Yet not only did Brendan befriend these individuals, but he managed to show others what good people they all were inside. It was incredible how he could expose the most interesting sides of people after knowing them for ten minutes. It's like he had some kind of magical way of bringing the best qualities out of anyone he ever met. Not only could he prove the worthiness of every individual, but he also proved his own worth along the way. You could be the cop arresting Brendan, but I promise you that ten minutes later you will be hysterically laughing and forming some special bond with him. Brendan could walk into a room of complete strangers and leave having a new group of friends. It was always so incredible how he could adapt to any situation.

Brendan taught me how to share. You will never meet a kid with fewer possessions or a lower sense of value for the things he owned. Although it may come off as a negative characteristic for someone to possess, he just proved how materialistic we all are. The simple belongings that we all fret about did not faze Brendan. As long as he had a shirt on his back and a place to sleep, he was set. You would never hear him complain about not having enough of anything, and the things he did own he was more than willing to share. Brendan was notorious for never having any money. I cannot even remember the number of times I bought him food, paid his way, or gave him money. There was one point in time when he did have some money, and the only thing he wanted to do was give it to me. During this period, he was constantly calling me, asking me if I needed any money. That Christmas, he took his money and bought me a sweater and two necklaces, and I have never felt a greater sense of pride coming from him than when he gave those gifts. He was so excited that he actually told me what he had gotten me weeks before Christmas even came.

Brendan taught me how to relax. It is so incredibly easy to let life get us worked up about the insignificant details. Even something as simple as getting to the bank after it closes can get us so angry that it ruins the rest of our day. I do not think that anything could ruin Brendan's day. Any time I was stressed out and turned to Brendan to tell him about my mishaps, his response was. "Who cares?" And he did not ask this because he did not care what I was talking about, but he asked to make me realize that these misfortunes did not matter. It was not worth having a bad day over a closed bank. It was not worth spending time sweating the small stuff. He had such an incredible way of making people take a step back to realize what was really important in life. Brendan's instant messenger screen was WWBD, "What Would Brendan Do." Although he created this to be humorous, I take it in full seriousness. Many times I have found myself in situations where I am confused about how to feel or what decision to make, and the easiest way for me to conquer this is by considering what Brendan would do in that situation.

Brendan taught me how to enjoy every moment of life. Awkward family gatherings were always so much easier when I had Brendan there to entertain me through the day. He could turn any situation into a great time. A few summers ago I babysat for a family nine hours a day, five days a week. For the low cost of five dollars a week, Brendan came with me every day to that job. He could have easily gotten his own job making much more money, but instead he tagged along with me to keep me company and to enjoy the summer together.

For leading such an atypical life, I was always so proud to talk about my brother and to brag to others about what a character I was blessed to have in my family. Not only was he the best brother I could have ever asked for, but he was my best friend. No one has ever known more about me or understood me more deeply than he. I have lost the person who was able to teach me my most valuable life lessons.

Brendan's life smarts and resilience were tested by a troubled relationship with his biological mother, who left the family through divorce when he was 11. Tim moved to an old house 40 miles south of Rochester, in the village of Mt. Morris, NY. Tim recalls:

Brendan thrived in this environment, the town was small, and Brendan had befriended the local antiques merchants; always stopping in and checking on what the current value was on his latest find. He also had a paper route with close to 400 customers. Every Friday after school Brendan would head over to the newspaper office and assemble his delivery for Saturday morning. Saturday I would meet Brendan at the office and help him deliver all 400 copies of the Mt. Morris Penny-Saver. Brendan saved enough money to buy himself an ATV, where he would spend hours exploring the back roads and woods of the area surrounding our town.

Our neighbor Mo became somewhat of a surrogate mom to Brendan. On the days she was off work, she would have milk and cookies waiting for him. Whatever may have troubled him that day, he would leave Mo's house with the biggest smile on his face, and not a care in the world. Mo and her husband, Joe, were frequently called on to watch Brendan when I needed to travel for business. He loved those overnight stays.

During the winter I started a major remodeling project that revealed that the house was collapsing and we needed to move. Brendan is uprooted again.

Brendan's difficulty in adjusting to the split, which was very messy, to his mother's rejection, and repeated moves resulted in difficulties in school, acting out, and the beginnings of depression and self-medication with pot.

It was from this point that Brendan seemed to spiral. Even though he was extremely bright, his behavior was starting to deteriorate. I was receiving daily calls from school, and daily in-school suspensions became the norm. If you were to look at Brendan in grades 8-12, four quarters per grade, he actually had three outstanding quarters to his credit, mainly due to his being high.

Over the next few years, Brendan took to writing out his frustrations:

My Mom
My own mom fucked me over. I guess I'm just an object to her. She looks at me and sees money. She doesn't see her son, her own flesh and blood. I risked my relationship with my dad to be with her. And this is what I get. I should have known. Dad was right. Right now there's only one way out. But they're watching me closely. If I had a BOOM! That's how quick I'd do it. People always say, "Oh, but you would miss out on so many things." Why would I care if I was dead? The only thing that's holding me back is my Dad and sis. She says she wants me to get help. She just wants me out of her life.

At 16, he was arrested for unauthorized use of a motor vehicle as an unlicensed driver, and driving after dark without an adult. He spent three days in the county jail. The same year he went to rehab for substance abuse—typically marijuana, cocaine, or alcohol—and failed due to behavior issues after one week. He returned later for one month and was released. He subsequently entered the PINS program and was court ordered to attend rehab, but this also failed, as Brendan could not adjust to this facility, and they were not equipped to handle such cases. The arrest and rehab had been initiated by Brendan's dad in an attempt to save his son. Given his age, Brendan saw this as a betrayal, going to live with his mother before moving back to live with his dad and sister within six months. By 17, Brendan was arrested for drug possession and once again, kicked out of outpatient rehab on suspicion of selling drugs during rehab sessions.

His record sheds further light on some of Brendan's rather humorous criminal leanings. In 2006, he was arrested for obstruction. Apparently Brendan was giving a colorful commentary of the arrest that was taking place below his balcony. According to Brendan's telling of the story, he was then charged with dropping cans out of his apartment window to the homeless on the street below.

This was followed by a claim that he was guilty of destroying private property when caught dancing on a Porta-potty.

Throughout this time, Brendan found an outlet in writing. His experiences in lock up and rehab took on a life of their own, feeding his fertile imagination with images of thugs and street life and gun culture that were not a part of his personal life. Despite his complete lack of experience with guns or pimps or hard time, he compensated by writing out his frustration and bravado in mimicked street language, painting a picture of cool and control. The persona throughout much of his work boasts a knowledge and experience that were far from Brendan's reality, but the technique aided him in seeking his place in the world. The fantasy world of street crime and gangster culture made way for the vulnerable teenage boy who was fighting his way through the complexities of family and romance. Brendan's imagery of women is complex and filled with anger and need in equal doses.

Melodramatic teenage angst is balanced with a delicate curiosity and astute assessment of the machinations of grown-ups—and growing up.

In the last year of his life, Brendan's ambition had been to attend culinary school, with an eye to someday opening a restaurant with his sister. With that dream in mind, Brendan held jobs in a few of the local restaurants, as well as a nearby bakery. He was finally beginning to imagine his life.

Leighanne, Tim's fiancée and Brendan's stepmom (whom he called Smommy), had found common ground with Brendan in the kitchen.

> *I first met Brendan when he was about 13 years old. He came with his Dad to meet a few friends for lunch. Those beautiful blue eyes and dimples were just too much. He was so good that afternoon, and little did I know that he would one day mean so much to me. But fast forward 4 years later when Brendan was working at the local bakery and was getting up at 5:30 in the morning every weekend and days off from school to go and work. I remember thinking, "I couldn't do that, let alone a 17 year old kid?" But he did, and he loved it. He'd come home and talk about the things he made, and there was such pride in his voice when he'd tell you about the bakery. Even when the bakery had to let him go due to declining business, Brendan still kept his love of cooking and it expanded over time. While he continued to work in the volatile food industry, he'd always come home talking about the new things he learned, new recipes he invented. Sometimes, if we were lucky, he'd share them with us. He would also make dinner for us as a special treat and it was always guaranteed to be delicious. If Brendan was home, then he was cooking for someone, at his or her request.*

> *That was one of the many things that so impressed me about Brendan—his love of cooking, along with his love of family. Brendan admired his father on so many levels. I just loved*

watching the two of them together. Brendan was always learning from his Dad. Whether it was opening the door for his girlfriend, as he had seen his father do for me, or asking his Dad to look at a car, he respected his Dad and they shared many great life moments that I was privileged enough to witness. I was impressed with their unwavering bond. I would just love watching Brendan and his Dad sit there and just laugh over funny stories and jokes, each just trying to make the other laugh harder. I would just look at "My Barry Boys" and be so happy that I got to be a part of this family. And whenever Caitlin was home from college, it meant that the jokes and laughing only grew louder. Our family dinners on Sunday grew to be quite popular, as both the kids would bring home their friends and Brendan always brought his girlfriend. We'd just sit there catching up on life, laughing, but mostly it was just a chance to make sure that at least once a week we got to sit down as a family. In fact, it was during one of these family dinners when Brendan came home with a pair of earrings for me—just unexpected and out of the blue. But that was Brendan—always doing something unexpected.

It was the respect that Brendan always showed to me that had shown me I was more than his Dad's fiancée. If Brendan saw me making dinner, he'd offer to help, especially if there was chopping involved because his knife skills were so much better that mine. And he always complimented me on any dish or dessert I made. I remember cooking my very first turkey last year and after Brendan made his infamous mashed potatoes we sat down to a feast. Brendan could not stop talking about how great it was and how much he loved it. He always made me feel very special whenever we had dinner together, knowing that he worked at some very high-end restaurants but he still enjoyed the meals we had on our table.

Brendan's creativity finally had an outlet that was positive and giving and true to his nature. Making meals for the family filled a need in him to be helpful and to nourish his relationships with those who understood him best. No doubt his family felt the love and promise of this endeavor, and believe he would have flourished.

The poems in this collection are also a testament to the power of Brendan's imagination to create something tangible from a cauldron of compulsions and obstacles, both hardwired and societal. Consider the following poems much as you would testing recipes. In them, Brendan was testing himself, trying to discern what combinations of personality, drive, and focus would result in the best person he could be. By conjuring up, exploring, keeping or discarding ingredients, he would no doubt have created a masterpiece.

Brendan Timothy Barry
March 8, 1987-June 3, 2007

Boy Stumbles

This is a story about a boy who stands after he stumbles
When the battle starts, he's always on the inside of the rumbles
I am not saying he is Superman, I see how he struggles
Mixed feelings thoughts questions somehow he juggles
Whatever the contender, he always finishes the scuffles
Right when he thought he had everything figured out, he ran
    into more troubles

See, what happened was
The boy got greedy with money, and got caught in a crime
Through that action he knew he was going to do time
No big deal, he was tough enough, he could do it on his head
At least in the beginning that is what he said
Until, he thought, he met the perfect girl
She jump started his life, and made it begin to whirl
I mean, before her, he was blind with no sight
He was stuck in a dark tunnel, and she gave him the light

They were inseparable, never would you see one without the
    other
He showed her more love, respect, and attention than his own
    mother
However, he tried not to let that secret escape
Because if the truth was revealed, the two would be in rough
    shape
So he treated her like a normal person
Denying his feelings, so he wouldn't be hurting
See the weight he was holding was too big for his frame
So he dumped the baggage, shared his thoughts, and did it
    with no shame
She responded well and was glad he did it
See, the girl swore she was in love, too bad she couldn't live it

Well, June 2nd came, and it was just another night in court
With him came her, she was there to support
The judge ended a case, then called out his name
He left her side not knowing, they would never be the same
See, what happened was
Up at the stand, the talks turned to pleas
They metaled him up, now the courtroom he leaves
While placed in a holding cell, she races through his mind
All the great past memories start to rewind

As they soon take control, he is walked out to the white van
He sees the one who gave him life before he's placed in the
hands of the white man
He's not so worried because he has court in four days
Well, the tables turned on him, so in jail he stays
While he tries to prepare himself for the 6 month bid
He starts reflecting and regretting all the stupid things he did
Plus trying to keep the acceptance from her he was feeling
And his parents were bribing, to see who would be child
support reeling
His main mission was to keep her at heart
Doing everything in his power, not to let separation make them
part
The mornings brought promises, letters, see that's when the end
just started to begin
Anxious for visits, but all her saw was the seat she used to sit in
And when he called her house, she was never home
Commitments were now broken, he was in it all alone
He hated getting her mail, because he could smell her perfume
and feel her presence
I'm telling you, he wouldn't have taken the plea if her knew all
this was part of the sentence

And the funny thing is

She knew about the charges and time before they were together

She swore up and down she could make it through any kind of weather

It's really too bad she couldn't live up to what she said

A month into his bid and the girl of his dreams had fled

He is lost now, but he will be more when he leaves

And when he gets the courage to look her in the face, a mask is all he sees

He came to the conclusion

Females are devils, but see they hide their horns

Using beauty as distractions, like rose buds from thorns

He also admits putting himself out the way he did was a big mistake

Recognizing he was a sucker, because he believed the fake

He believed all her promises, and dreamed what they could be

Off in Lalaland, so the happy ending is all he could see

Alone with his broken family, him losing his girl was salt on the cut

So he starts receiving acceptance letters from other girls, to help heel the wound shut

He still stays thinking and planning of ways to get her back
Until the day he figured why he wants her so bad
See, it's human nature to want what you can't have
So he moved on realizing she is just one of the many fish in the sea
Let go of the past to prepare for what the future will be
In addition, every mistake made he will learn from
The next time he will be patient for the right girl to come

Home Sweet Home

I wish I could have
A home sweet home
Instead
Snowstorm
Locked out
I'm all alone
Sweater on my back
Cold with no phone
Staring at the warm dog
Who will always have a home
Have a bed
2 times a day
he's guaranteed to be fed
Puppies and People
Shouldn't be treated equal
I should come first
Instead Reggie's 10 levels above
That little shit
Receives more attention, respect, and love
Than I'll ever get
That was just a sample
Not good enough?
Here's another example
Divorce happens
Now Mommy's on the rebound
Needs a guy with cash
By the pound
Found him

Proceeds to erase us
Years later
Has the nerve to face us
Not a hint of remorse
Has ever been shown
And you wonder why
For 6 years
You've been alone
Happy you always
Put us last?
Future doesn't look so promising
So I put you in my past
You'll be in the back row
Of my graduation
And as far as marriage
Don't expect an invitation
I hope that saying about
Marrying your own mother
Isn't true
I'll wind up killing her
Thinking it was you
It's so sad to see
The stories you tell the family
Like Reggie's still barking
And we're still talking

She Never Knew Me

I did everything I could
To be with you
And what did my bearer do?
Threw it back in my face
So fuck you, too
Bearer,
You used me to get your fix of money
Like Pooh Bear uses beehives
To get his fix of honey

Written two page letters
Trying to incarcerate me to the judge
This is just gonna prolong this hate and grudge
It's all making sense now
Your needed me on your side
So you fought for me at Park Ridge
I'm hoping the next dry season we have
I hope you're jumping head first
off the local canal bridge
Did I really make your life corrupted
crazy
and wild
I know grown women
who know my troubles
have families
children
and still begging for me to be their next child
now that's crazy

You and your roomie are fucked
and lazy
Trying to be manipulators
But are horrible at what you do
Your life is shitty
so everyone's life around
you has to be shitty too
trying for an emancipation
I'm your own blood
A true creation

This is the reason I didn't use Mom in this
because Mom means mother
mother means lover
no love was shown
So we can't look back and say
wow, this relationship has grown
all I wanted was love
a simple kiss on the forehead
and a true hug
but that won't happen

That's sad
sad
pretty fucking sad
I have one support
I wish I had two
I know now the second will never be you

Whenever

You did whatever you had to
To produce that money
Put shelter over my head
Clothes on my back
And food in my tummy
Even when you were on the edge
Of being starving
And hungry
Through the bad
You stuck by my side
Supported
And was true
When you said that you loved me
Whenever I was out of line
You was always there
Whenever I was locked up
You would make bail
And get me out of jail
Whenever you found empty baggies
You'd believe whatever I said
Since then
The devil's gotten sick
And the devil's almost dead
But it takes time to change
So I'ma go at my own pace
But at the end of time all behaviors
Pain, hurt will erase

You'll know when that day comes
Cause you'll see it on my face
When you had no hesitation
Made sure I was on time to every place
You were there and gave
Whenever I messed up
You encouraged me
To admit
The mistakes I've made
Whenever I tried to be sneaky
Deceitful or move in stealth
You were right there
You know me
Better than I know myself
Whenever I need to know something
You always told me
Whenever I got neglected
Open arms
You were there to hold me
Whenever I was teary
You would wipe my eyes
I truly am sorry
For all the lies
You would always look through the bad
And see good too

You didn't do it because
That's what a parent should do
You did it because you are true
Sometimes I don't believe when you say
There was no dad for you
Then how did you know
What a good father's supposed to do
Like you say
It gets worse
Before it gets better
I'm just saying it
Not trying to use it as a lever
Whenever you would say
Things well be ok
Someday
I believe, I believe

Perfect

No stress on my crown
I peacefully count the sheep
I wake up from a deep sleep
Crepes cooking
I'm hungry
Pull out my chair
And sit down
The table that now
Has 4 sitting around
Confused but I sit
Not noticing everyone's smiling
With their faces well lit
For once there's 4 of us
Cleaning up the mess
Take one pill
Cause the other was for stress
Perfect smell
Perfect feeling
Perfect lighting
The other mom hot
Both parents
But I hear no fighting
Never did I think waking
Could be so exciting
Heading out the door

I give them both a hug
For that short moment
I finally felt real love
Leaving stress free
Without a thing on my mind
Finally able to smoke
Without the worry of the rewind
See. when everything's gone
It's the simple shit you miss
Like me staying our of trouble
And Dad giving Mom a kiss

Betrayal

Have you ever been hated or discriminated against
I have
I've been denied, violated and put to the test
Kicked out of every place I've ever lived in
All cause I kick up dirt like a pig in a pen
Plus every move I make they consider a sin
Still hold my head up high, and carry a grin
It's my mother, she's not yours, she's mine

I'm tired of you both feeding me these bullshit lines
I love you, son, we'll always be together
You're a fake ass bitch
Like pleather is to leather
And Phil I just want to bang that bald head against the walls
Hit in the stomach, good kick in the balls
It's just one of the many sick dreams I often have
I love it, cause I can wake up, look at his ugly mug, and laugh
It's the only way I can whoop his ass and not wind up in jail

Been moving more than U-Haul truck
But I'm at the end of my rope
Throwing my hands up to God, like what the fuck
Being kicked out in the middle of a snowstorm
Mom, don't you remember 16 years ago
When we were in the hospital and I was being born
Probably not
Cause they gave you the anesthetic shot
I wish you would have never woke up from it

Rewind

My life reminds me of a VCR
When I wanna rewind
I've gone too far
When I wanna fast forward
Got to sit and wait
Give myself to the Lord
Cause I'm under His fate
His stay
His pay
His rate
Will all this shit forever last?
Am I the only one
Who's present is my past?
17 years traveling this lonely path
Only to be discovered and swallowed
By the dark wrath
Maybe it's because I think
The right is wrong
Or maybe cause I let the blunt be my light
See, the trouble blinds me
But the freedom gives me my sight
People say duck down
But I stand up

A prime example
Of why I fuck up
Cause I listen and trust only me
Could it be
I was abused, abandoned, rejected, locked and set free?
Is that the reason I act up?
Probably
Dumb ass is a crack baby, could figure me
Instead Dad drops bucks on a PhD
Don't you know that diploma doesn't mean shit
Cause when the session's over
Memories fresh I could never forget
So I cover it with smiles and laughs
As I continually walk down
These lonely dark paths

My Life as a Car

My life with you reminds me of a modern day car
A rust bucket body, but the power to go far
As I travel this journey over different terrain and rubble
The ride's smooth for six months, but somehow I run into
    trouble
Cause in my rearview mirror I see my mistakes
I say, "Fuck the past" and hit the gas instead of using the brakes
That's when I hit a pothole, lose control, and my roof meets the
    ground
Unable to repair so 4 months I rest in the pound
No one wants to pay so I'm towed to a junkyard where I sit as
    a reject
Until this mechanic sees a diamond in the dirt, and came to
    collect
She pulled me out of the mud where I left big ruts
She tuned my engine, fixed my exhaust which put an end to the
    putts
She didn't stop there, no, her heart told her to do more
Swapped out the old frame and dropped a new floor
She patched, sanded, buffed every square inch of rust
Took her time with the primer, cause a good paint job was a
    must

Now it's like a brand-new mobile in tiptop condition
Burning rubber with doughnuts, and quick when it comes to
lane switchin'
It was a good seven months without any faults or mistakes
Until August rolled around, then it had another malfunction
with the brakes
Now I sit in the shop waiting, while she's debating if she's
gonna fix it or not
Her last two cars failed on her the same way, so what's this one
got?
She gives him one more chance for him to fail
He feels threatened by a new owner, like he's going up for sale
But he sees it as they got through this storm they can get
through any weather
See . . . Every time the engine's running, they're riding together
And when the car sits, he prays he'll have the same owner
forever

Turning Twelve

All my actions
you could interpret them wrong
I feel
If you could sell yourself
My life I'd pawn
A year
A week
A day
I wish I could live it
If you didn't kill yourself
You'd drug to forget it
It's like
I try to do right in the eyes
But the wheel won't steer
I've had this problem
For the last 6 years
The skin I wear
I try to fit it
Spewing out my thoughts and feelings
And nobody can get it
Day I turned twelve
I was put on the bud list

That little bastard
A future molester
Gangster
He's our next terrorist
Let's push him to death
He won't be missed
Jump on his feelings
Then lock him with a razor
Till he slits his wrist
But that won't happen
No
I got goals and power behind this heart
The opportunity is coming
Just watch me dart
And when I do
I'm gonna come back to this place
So this so-called terrorist
Can see the look on your face

Girl of My Dreams

Girl of my dreams, what she has is true
Petite with a big heart standing 5'2"
Sparkling eyes, hair of all brown shades
And a smile that brightens all of my days
This girl's beauty no one comes close to even compare
She can make riots quiet then stop and stare
They say don't judge a book by its cover
This girl's outside plus reading makes it hard not to love her
I want this dream to never ever end
Because what I have is a girl, plus a best friend
She accepts my flaws, and cherishes what's good
Going above and beyond what a girlfriend should
She takes me in roughed up and muddy
Not together, but by my side like a best buddy
She gives me all the needed love and support
Like filling up the chair next to me every time I'm at court
Her visits give me the energy not to lose the battles in the fear
I hold on thinking of her till the next time

I want to see her more than my own family
Being love-struck, that's my new reality
Feelings being felt I never could feel
Maybe a good pinch could let me know if it's real
To be honest, continuing in this dream forever, glad I'd be
Not ever wanting to open my eyes to stop the fantasy
And you wouldn't either, if you were in my place
You too, would never lose sight of that special face
I need peace around me, so I can continue dreaming
Outrageous fantasy but I believe what I'm seeing
Because what I see I know it has to be true
Johnna, this dream girl, you should know that it's you

Kristen

You're that fantasy girl
I would always see in my dream
Everything I'm about to say to you
I truly do mean
It was the first Thursday in December
The next day I was off to Conifer
If I correctly remember
You gave me your address
And said, "You better write to me"
When I was there I think I wrote 3
Or was it 4
I coulda shoulda woulda wrote more
But I never knew then
That God would give me such a great gift to have
Or should I say had
I never knew you could miss someone this bad
I'm not even gone yet
And I already miss you
That's how I know this love is true
We've been through rough tides
And had our tough times
Like when you would take the razor to your leg and sever

I don't want you to go out like that
I want to grow old and die together
Just like the scientist
I'm going to take us back to the start
So we can remember the good times
Before I part
It was December 29
From that day I've been yours and you've been mine
January 6 sitting on the loveseat
Funny that's where our love muscles happened to meet
That day I stole that one time special something from you
Same day you stole my heart so I stole yours, too
The 13th of January
That was the day you flipped out about me
Through the tears and bloodshed, love I did see
I went from I love you
To I'm in love with you
So much love
I don't know what to do
That night your point was so strong
Girl, I love you when you're right
I love you

Missy's Valentine

It was a muggy July 4th
AKA Independence Day
Decision was mine
I was ready to accept any consequences headed my way
No words could have held me back and made me stay
I was so sick and tired of feeling numb
So I called up Justin and said, "Here I come"
Sunday was good
But Monday was better
Nobody could have prepared me for what I was about to see
Waking up from a bad trip
Staring into the eyes
Of a girl named Missy
Suddenly reality hit me
Not knowing what to do
I started to clean the room of Nicki
Trying to clear my head
I had to figure out the feelings within me
So we started talking and joking
Found out nothing was fake
Should I kiss her or not
A decision I had to make
It was time to go

So I grabbed you and gave you a hug
On the way home I was telling Carolina
She's cute and her personality I love
A day goes by, we start talking at 11
Our conversation ended, 2 hours short of 7
2 days later, you did the jaw-dropping stunt
I couldn't have asked for more
I've known you for 4 days
And you're already at my door
Something about you stuck in my head
Probably a combination of the actions you've done
And the words you've said
I've known you 5 days
Yet I know everything about you
Like the hate you're feeling
I can relate to what you're going through
Every time we talk, it draws me closer to you
I really want Missy and Brendan to be we
You might think this is a corny way to say it
But will you go out with me?

Listen to the Sweet Heart

I thought you were real, from day one you were a fake
Still a little girl, so you pass the blame
Like it was someone else's mistake

Getting out of school and going nowhere in life
You should have taken advantage of the situation
Of being someone's wife

Really, no, how to fuck up when it's smooth and good
Group made me think you thugging
Straight from the hood

5 foot, maybe 5 foot 1
Has it occurred to you
Weighing a tenth of a half ton

And that's soaking wet
Saying you can fuck up Carol
Bitch, I bet

All you can do is create problems, never fix 'em
Your own pop doesn't wanna see you
So the bags he packs, then ships 'em

I thought that would be a wake-up call, some reality check
Totaling relationships
Unfixable wreck

Maybe if you started listening to the sweetheart
Stopped to listen to your fucked up thoughts
You wouldn't see this relationship part

Don't take my words as trying to be demeaning
I'm trying to get through to you,
Not trying to get even

How Come?

How come?
We don't even talk no more
We're barely on the phone at all
It feels like there's no love
Shown at all
And now there's tears coming
Down your face
It's my fault
I made the mistakes

How come?
You can't put yourself in my place
I wish all bad would just erase
Still stuck in the house
With an ankle bracelet you dislike
But my ankle hates it
When you come I can appreciate it

How come?
We're ten days shy
To let the first month go by
Greatest thing that's happened to me, no lie

So how come?
You pick apart the smallest shit
Type of stuff you should dust off
And just forget
Sit there and dwell
And act like things are all well

So how come?
I feel like you don't want this to last
Acting like I'm a BF of the past
An asshole in the make
Feelings I've felt
Shit hasn't been fake

So how come? Huh? How come??

Karina

I don't know how to start this
With the ink-n-pen
I'm a threw everything out
So let me begin
I think back now
And know jail was a must
Through the negative experience
I gained a positive plus
If it wasn't for Anthony
There would be no Karina
If it wasn't for rehab
Who knows when I would have seen ya
But it happened
And I'm glad it did
First thoughts were
"That girl's too skinny to have had his kid"
Had to throw that joke
Somewhere inside my rhyme
My true thought was
I have to make her mine
Became a full time job
Towards the end

Thought it was a waste of time
Cause you started doing your own thing
I thought you were gone forever
Days became cloudy
I'd see rays of sun
But that didn't change the weather
I was sick of living my days down and blue
So you pushed the clouds aside
And let your love shine through
For once I found a girl that was true
Karina, if you don't know
That girl was you
If I ever said I wasn't in love
Know now I lied
You're in my life now
So stick by my side
Cause you're the one when
I'm upset, depressed or angry
You can erase my frown
When it comes time for August
You should know I'm down
It's not even June
And I don't hear from you any more

But you're still the girl I'll always be down for
I page, call
And no response back
Is it love, interest, or time that you lack?
Can't even give me the time of day
To tell me that
I guess Usher was right
When said to me "You got it bad"
These short conversations
Shit's making me sad
Number one priority
So you're the girl I'd call for
One of a kind
Type of girl anyone could fall for
But if there's no feelings no more
I don't wanna lose you as a friend
Do you really want to throw everything out
And let this relationship end?
Before you decide to walk
Pick up the phone
Cause between you and me
We really need to talk

Can't Believe

Can't believe you could ever do this
Can't believe I could say
You're fuckin useless
A fruit that won't ripen
A flower that won't bloom
Well, maybe it's early
Maybe too soon
See, I don't have energy nor the time
To have your tarnish steal my shine
Never wanted to be like one
Who in herself couldn't spot a flaw
But future phrase coming
"It's all about me, duh"
A self-centered who could never think of another
I did say I would never marry my mother
So I'm glad everything worked out so right
So glad you're out of sight
So glad I don't have to dial
Just to say fuckin good night
God does have a plan
We could be walking hand in hand
Through the sand

Glare in each other's eyes
Together like Siamese twins
Attached at the sides
You're mine
And I am your
Biggest fan
I'm glad that wasn't His final plan
See, I'm gonna do bigger and better things with my life
I'm not gonna be strapped with a girl
Who wants the role of a wife

It's Sick

It's sick, but who could ever predict
3 years later
and still doing the same shit
you say you're doing it for me but you don't
you do it for you
it's true
too late I've lost all trust
just every other guy
I beat it till I bust
Ream each other out
We know what it's about
Wild dreams of me
Throwing you on the couch
Punches in the mouth
Dreams ends when I knock your ass out
Like always
Apologize after
Laughter, lies, and pain
It's insane
Then we're back to the same road again

It's sad but it's true
When I'm laying with you
There ain't nothing anyone could ever say or do
But when it comes down to it
I still hate you
Do you hate me?
Looking sexy and cute when you get worked up and angry
Sorry but the beauty can't change me
It just makes me wanna take you
And fuck
Like I don't even know you
You fuck other people
I fuck other people

A Simple Detour

I knew a beautiful Ashley, we met at seven
Shared the same classes, went our own ways at 11
Kept my eye on her in middle school
She was a straight edge, never bent a rule
4 years went by and she was back to me
Not just once, I was seeing her daily
Until I started an argument, something stupid, I bet
I now regret the fact, I gave up and let go
My fault? I still don't know
Anyway, she stumbled into the wrong crew
They were far in the game, so they gave her the wrong brew
No one could stop what she had started
Not even the old group, they all parted
These devils had her riding in whips
Put her onto glass till she fell through the crack
Now she's riding dicks, getting money for licks
Just to fulfill a fix, shit makes me sick

Well, years go by, I'm city shopping at the flea market
I feel a tap on the shoulder, I was someone's target
I'm now staring into the eyes that used to light rooms in the
    past
Only thing I see them lighting now is rocks in the glass
Tens, twenties, she goes through 'em fast
Now she lives in a dope house, with an unsmokable mass
I say it all, no emotional response, just a glossing glare
Followed by an empty, lonely dark stare
Her head, how can I get to it?
Reached in my pocket, got out the wallet
This is a picture were you were fifteen
Look what you've made of yourself, now a big fiend
A year shy of twenty
A mother with no house, still tricking for money
Suddenly her teardrops turned to severe panic cries
Well, I wiped her cheeks, gave my address, and said goodbye
Brief thoughts like, "Is she still hitting rocks?"
Till 2 months later when I hit the mailbox
Ashley was on the envelope, Park Ridge in the corner
Good, I think, she's out of dope

I read, "I've been here a month and I've already grown
Hardest thing I had to do was give Maria a better home
That was the thing that hurt the worst
See, I stopped being selfish and put her first
You saw my faults and made it clear you could spot them
You made me see the last of my rock bottom
The favor you did I could never repay
So from this day on sober I'll stay."
See, the simple reach out
Made this dying flower do a 360 and peek out
I learned some people don't know what's real
Till it's said to their face
Days can go by till it's set into place
Things will change, they won't be what they were
But it has to happen with a simple detour
A simple detour to show what is wrong
A simple detour to show what you once had is now gone
But see, it's never gone back to the point where you can't get it
    back
Even if you have another run in with the devil called crack
No matter how deep you've dug yourself in land
Because there will always be a shovel in reach of a hand

The Medical Healer

I ain't no city boy
I'm a suburban dealer
Known to the white kids as the medical healer
Take a hit of this and there be no question why it's bad
It will put you into a wheelchair like Superman
If you ain't buying from me I'm running your pockets
Pull out the heater, I'm shooting out rockets
Even with your matrix skills you can't stop it
When I roll, I roll with a 'matic
Have your whole crew in a panic
I went from weed to coke to 'shrooms to crack
Never thought I'd stab my best friend in the back

Verses

I can spit four rhymes
Before you can snort 2 lines

I'm not talking, I'm just stating facts
Like you use your 2nd set of eyeballs to watch our backs

I say beef is silly
Till it comes down to the tech 9 mills

And mamas be crying
Cause her son's a-dying

They wanna move up in the world but they can't
Cause they solve a problem by busting out the gate

Pulling out the heat
In the middle of the street

Killing innocent kids
If they ain't dying of bullets, they're dying of SIDS

We got killers, pimps, and STD infested feins
We got drugs, guns, and murder scenes

See shit like this at such a young age
They don't know how to grow up and turn the page

So they stick it in the back of their mind
When the drugs run out they have to rewind

Go looking for some stolen properties
Get a few guns and do a coupla robberies

Fill my lungs with the crack smoke
Hold it till I start to choke

So close to passing out
Getting fucked up is what I'm all about

Before

I'm sick of coming to forks in roads
And always steering the wrong way
I do what I wanna do
And say what I wanna say
You can accept
Or reject
It's your decision
Not mine
I'm on a road of self-destruction
In my mind
Shit's still fine
Who's to say I can't hit this
Or blow this line
Who?
You
You're just my p/o
So get the fuck out of my way
Like I said before
I do what I do
And say what I say
Put me behind bars I'll change

Take me out I'm the same
I played you all
So I'm champ of this game
I did what I had to do
Goddam it I did it
So instead of being on the inside
I got my clothes-n-fittin
Masterminded by a 16-year-old
You're all a bunch of suckasses
I'll smoke when I wanna smoke
And see how my luck goes
Don't like
Well, get usta me
Those are my thoughts
Of what I usta be

Blast 2 the Past

I wish now I could blast 2 the past
Because the write-up in Wayne Times
Will forever last
So put yourself in my place
Trying to get revenge
You run up in a crib
And grab a pint from the case
Now you get a petty larceny
and burr under you waist
Bounce out not getting too far
Next thing you know
You're in the back of a cop car
No time to sit and sip on Budweiser
No time to sit back, relax and party
So now you're in cuffs
At the police station
Pigs breathing down your neck
Threatening incarceration
So you fold
Give him his reports
Won't see me on the basketball courts

Because I'm on my way to jail
Last stop
The judge
And he won't set bail
Strip me down
Put me in the shower
Gave me some wash to get the lice out
No windows in this shithole
Can't even see if it's nice out
Blinded by the flash
They've taken mug shots
Cold cell
3 sheets
And rough cots
So I'm sitting on my back
Staring at the ceiling
Figuring our what's my true life's meaning
Deciding if this life is really worth leaving

Doing Time

I've been in plenty of rehabs and jails
So I got my share of stories and tales
Cellblock sitting
No money for bail
By my own mother
I was set up to fail
She wasn't about to stop and breathe
Till she saw her own blood in jail
See, I'm like time
I can't be changed
When I wanna rewind
It's too late
And when I wanna fast forward
I have to sit back and wait
So I put my hands in His
Cause He chooses my fate
You can just listen to this
Or you can listen and relate
I can look at anyone now
And see a bit of me
If you're at the beginning
Of your downfall
You're too high to ignore it
and too blind to see

Career Criminal College

Jail is the university of becoming a career criminal
It brings loopholes of the law to your subliminal
During your semester you'll sit and plan the next big crime
Blue printing your operation, so never again will you do time
You'll learn making money on a misdemeanor like weed is lame
You should step your game up and be one with cocaine
And if you really want to be on top, you should slang of
    Montego
But be sure to spend less than ten grand if you want to lay low
Cause if you spend anymore the IRS will be hot on your trail
And these federal crimes come with a very high bail
So while you're out there splurging and spending your g's
You should put a stash away for bail and lawyer's fees
When it comes to holding cannons, you should just say fuck it
Here you'll learn to pay a fine, to take a rap and tuck it
Cause nobody in their right mind wants to do an eight-month bid
And it could be longer if it holds a body that someone else did
So take my advice and know when you get chrome thirsty
Unless your plan is to be chowing down on the two-toned
    turkey

Also you'll find a while shit load of connections
Thieves, fiends, dealers, whole shitload of selections
You'll find out whose crack is cut, and whose caine is raw
You'll learn the names of informers who work for the law
When you leave, you'll know all the locations of chop shops in
    the hood
You'll have the numbers of hustlers who treat their customs as
    best as they should
Be sure to get the addresses of feins, cause once a fein always a
    fein
You'll be selling to your Bunkie
Wait, you got to be accepted here to see what I mean
And once you are, this puzzle will fit into place
See, if you apply what you learn, you can laugh law in the face
Because you'll be getting out of charges by beating every case
So if criminal school sounds good to you
The entry test is easy. Commit a crime or two.

Ear Piercing

Ear piercing vocals can make a brick house crumble
But shout in the King's face, or you'll get lost in the jungle
See, where I'm from
The noisier you get, the more scared you are
Raising your voice in here only gets you so far
People make a racket to get the dep to squash the beef
And the eyes peeling the situation know the shouter's a pussy
     under
All those tattoos, the war stories, the battle scars
Get behind these walls, there is always someone tougher than
     you are
A rowdy mouth is like a bluffer in a poker game
See if you have the money behind the muscle you can dead his
     name
Put an end to their word fame
Because everyone knows actions are louder than words
The way to describe panic by sound waves is fucking absurd
Crazy, insane, shocking, so outrageous
A booming mouth is like strep, it's so contagious
Monkey see, monkey do, they see, but avoids a wind up
But keeping the quick approach and you'll really end up in a
     line up

See people flap their lips as warning
Like beavers smack their tails
But nine out of ten times
The follow through always fails
Because they're scared to swing their arms and feel a little pain
Maybe they shout just to keep they're little bit of sane
But the bottom line is
Raising your voice in here only gets you so far
The noisier you get, the more scared you are

Got No Money

Listen, I got no money, and I got no name
I can kill two birds with a stone in the hustler's game
Starting out, I need cookies the size of a clam
I'm not talking messaging but I can sure telegram
So don't try to get me, don't dare try to rip
Please, please, don't let the thought cross you of trying to stick me
Like Bobby does Whitney, you'll get slapped pretty quickly
But it won't be a hand, I'll make the situation sticky
Now you're lying there limp, you thought I was in it for fun
You'll live another day, it was just the butt of a gun
See what happened when you tried one on me, you were done, son
You tried to paly me for a sucker, I proved I'm not a dumdum
See that quick happening and I got me a name
Time to put in some work in the hustler's game

See I steal for money and a pretty product stash
In an hour, the bankroll got bigger, like a scratch with a rash
Time to chop and cut product and make that fast cash
Weighing a must so I pull a brick from my sash
1st brick reads 35-20, these measurements are hectic, man
But wait, my scale's got options, so I switch it to metric man
It reads 1000 grams, that's a fat kilo man
How can I get rid of this and still be low man
That's a question only time can tell
But see, I still got a brick in the bag, and one under the belt
Now I'm dreaming, like I'll keep two in flakes, the other I'll melt
No, wait, I will keep one brick in nose candy, the other I'll bubble
I feed the countryside with sniff and the yuk for the jungle
Feeling normal will be a fiend's daily struggle
No small falls this Cain will make them do a cliff jump stumble

Back to reality, man, I need to bag it quick
I wish I had the knowledge of what it was cut with
I'll let my nose be the tester with a swift sniff
Back of my throat's numb, I can feel it heading to my brain
Hands start shaking, it's taking control of my frame
This product's pure as can get, could this be true?
Must, cause I sniffed the first one a ¼ 10, now it's ¼ 2
4 hours, and 2 8 balls later

I'm starting at 3 bricks uncut, I cut in, what else could be
    greater
Heart's pounding, veins full of caine, I've been high for a while
Rail after rail and I haven't even put a dent in the pile
What am I doing?
Heat up the stove, it's time to cook the coke in the vile
Never been a chef, I couldn't handle pork-n-beans
But put me in the kitchen, and I'll show you the rise and fall of
    coke-n-dreams
The rise, that's when the fiends say you got 'em
The fall, that's when you try your own product and hit your
    rock bottom
But that's not me, I'll never hit that stage
Product's cooked, I can't believe I produced such a pretty shade
    of beige

I want to go cop a rose, but I can't let them know I'm tasting
    the rock, man
So I go to the fridge, chug a Pepsi, now I'm taking a hit with a
    pop can
No turning back, I wish I could stop, man
I will, I will, just one more blast
I've never seen two grams of cook disappear so fast
Fuck, it's only 400 bones of my profit's stash
I went to sleep and put that day in the past
Now I'm making calls trying to rid me of a brick
3 calls, 2 unanswered, I'm telling you, it can happen that quick
hop in the whip, pump the gas, I'm ready to drive
4 tracks, 15 minutes later my destination arrives
we talk, we debate, settle; now I'm up 19.5
I hit the car auction, now I'm riding in class
Money brings in bitches, so the shotgun bucket seats a fine ass
Teeth plated in gold, two diamond fronts clearer than glass
Apartments decked out, flat screens, Louie suits; it all screams
    out cash
And on top of it all I still got an unsmokable mass

Well, the days turned into weeks, the weeks switched the
    seasons
I try to break free of the crib, but I keep thinking of reasons
Like the cat's going to catch me, the cop's going to cuff me
I now look in the mirror and see I'm past the point of ugly
My body's withered to nothing like the Corpse of Salina
Crack's turned my life upside down, like families with Katrina
Started out with 3 bricks, now I'm down to a quarter
I was supposed to be a come-up man, not one with a disorder
See, back in the day I used to buy from the pawnshop
Now every time I'm in the building, stolen goodies I drop
Then I take the money to the spot for a quick cop
And on my way I pass the building I used to live in
It brings back memories, like the feeling of my body covered in
    silk and linen
Two nude girls in the bed smiling and grinning
Controlling the cravings, I tried to work at
It swallowed me whole; I'm still lost in the habit
In the beginning, I wanted money and a name, that's what I
    said
Now I'm broke, no money, and my found name has become a
    base head

Cruzin

Cruzin to Columbia
Coco cabanas
Robin Escaba
Sqeezin bananas
Clap them in hammers
Travelin back through the Panamas
Now got more kokis than Florida
Bitch is a schema
I hit her
While you holda
Records long
You gonna need more than a folda
New bitch I'll make and molda
Sit back let her do the hustle
Throw her a 9
She don't need the muscle
All she needs to be is trigger happy
Right Pappy?
I said Right, Pappy?

I chill while she puts the barrel under his chin
Do it
Clap he
I wasn't there
She take the rap for me
She takes away the court wait
And agony
Got her trained better than the pit on the leash
Got her paying $543 on the Jag lease
Never seen anyone flip faster kiss

Fantasy vs. Reality

Fantasies are how reality's depicted
That's why I criticize the critic
Life is something you can't enforce
Like a dying animal
You should let nature take its course
What's meant to be will be, you see
Don't ever try to alter reality
Still you try
Cause rapped up in your head's
This fake fantasy
So from this day on
No crack babies will be born
Divorce doesn't exist
Families can't be torn
Knives are for meat
No such thing as stabbing
Products get paid for
No five-finger grabbing
Gunpowder is unheard of
So explosions can't happen
We battle it out in chess
So there are no war street sagas
In teen pregnancies
Boys stay to be fathers

People have realized
Hard work gets you paid
No taxes taken out
From the money we made
No roaches or rats
Where we live in
White black yellow
You're an equal citizen
Sex isn't forced
No such word as rape
AIDS hasn't found
The horny little ape
Breast lifts, tummy tucks
There's no one to pay
How you were born
Is how you should stay
It's what's on the inside
That shows your true beauty
This is the same place where PMS
Doesn't make you moody
See, this place everyone's heart is clean
Not torn and muddy
Osama is my neighbor
And Adolph's my buddy

See, there's no sizzurp sipping
So there's no DWI
Revenge hasn't been born
No eye for an eye
Bloods and Crips combined
And became violet
The men comes aboard
And slaps hands with the pilot
No welfare or food stamps
Cause our pockets are humungous
We drink out of each other's cups
And not worry about lip fungus
No sniffles or coughs
We got the cure for the common cold
Con artists have real jobs
There's no robbing the old
DEA are just letters
Cause there's no dope
We never picked the stem up
Since there's no need to cope
No prison exists
So you can't drop the soap
Every child gets

His 'n her equal loving
Michael Jackson is known as a singer
And not the little boys he's touching
King and Gandhi are still alive
But never for the speak their great voice
People would accept responsibility
But nobody's made a bad choice
Joker's boy is Batman
And Superman's still flying
Babies don't get shook
They smile instead of crying
We are one big family
And we act like it, too
This fantasy world
Is so far from true!

I Believe

I believe in sneaking when you act a clown
I believe in stomping when a man is down

I believe in rolling cause I roll real tight
I believe in toking when the time is right

I believe in selling and making some cheddar
I believe in packing 2 Berettas

I believe your bark is louder than your bite
I believe you're dead if I catch you at night
I Believe

I believe in sneaking when you act a clown
I believe in stomping when a man is down

I believe in rolling cause I roll real tight
I believe in toking when the time is right

I believe in selling and making some cheddar
I believe in packing 2 Berettas

I believe your bark is louder than your bite
I believe you're dead if I catch you at night

Labels and Choices

Terrorist, terrorist
I could be one, too
I could jump in a plane maker with JetBlue
I can board with a terrorist
And shake hands with the pilot
Wait an hour or two
Then start a fatal riot
All you Americans
Get the fuck on the ground
Shut the fuck up
And stop moving around
Listen, I call the shots
. . . You hear
See those towers
Turn the wheel and steer
See, I hold the strings
I'm the puppet master
Now hit that fuckin tower
And die, you fuckin bastards
I can go with Allah
I've had my fun
Last day on earth
Was nine one one

Molester, Molester,
I could be one, too
I could chill at playgrounds
And look for little Booby or Sue
Carrying candy in one hand
And puppies in the other
I could be the babysitter
That gets paid by your mother
I could be that uncle
That touches
My nieces little brother
Bringing kites to the park
Ask if you wanna fly it
Or help me find my dog
Children always buy it
Going to such measures
To fulfill my sick pleasures
That was a secret
It wasn't supposed to be told
But the parents got concerned
And the truth did unfold
I was a mastermind

How could I get caught?
The threats I gave
I thought they all bought
Living with children
That was my vision
Not getting killed
While I waited for trial in prison

Gangster, Gangster
I can be one, too
I can hand out handkerchiefs
And call them for my crew
I could hustle shit
Save up money for a piece
Then when I go buy it
Stomp out in the streets
I'll take that one,
And that one, and that one, too
Then use your own gun
To get rid of you

Wait around the corner
For when the cops are due
Change their suits to maroon
Instead of dark blue
Headed home to soak my hands
For an hour or two
Should relax, relax
Bang, bang, on the door
The cops are coming through
Now I'm in cuffs
Like, what do I do?
They take away my colors
And put me in them suits
Give me Bruce Lees
I can't wear my boots
I ain't getting out of this one
Four counts of homicide
Should have answered die
Instead of ride
Now I'm in prison
Till my body rots
Last thing I felt was
Lethal injection shots

The lives lost to this
Are lives hard to miss
See, these are the profiles
That won't bring you far
They will bring you death
Or sitting behind bars
Bad decisions
You'll always have to pay
So don't sit and watch
Your life slip away

The Life of a Street Gun

I'm smuggled into the country, without any traces
Sold to anyone with cash, no matter what the race is
Only to have the government, absolutely despise us
Because I come with such power, in different shapes and sizes
Whatever piece needed, mu owner's got it in stock
What's your preference? Rifles, revolvers, or the unjammable
    Glock
I'm bragged about, like my clip can hold more
I'm thrown in people's faces, showing my owner's really
    hardcore
I get used by the ignorant who don't have a fucking clue
And once I leave the holster, it's not up to me what I do
See, it's never my fault. It's the person who gives that tiny
    squeeze
And after that it's out of my control, I'm forced to release
And where the lead goes, it's the holder's choice
I get equipped with silencers, to muffle my voice
See, the shots from me can make a jack man's chest melt
Like the burn of devil's spring vodka, the feel will get felt
And the blood will start flowing and going from the throat
Until it surrounds the body, now that's a man-made moat
And I would have gotten fired less, but I lacked the beam

On the winning side, so I got tucked, now I'm fleeing from the
    scene
And being in possession of me would be a holder's mistake
So the next thing I feel is the water, at the top of the lake
Now I will pass by the fish till I reach the silt
Finally being able to rust in peace, free from all the guilt
Cause no longer am I able to create any more holes
No longer am I able to push back any more souls
So years will pass, I'll probably be a scuba diver's prize
And the thought will never come to them that I used to take
    lives

I Once Knew a Man

I once knew a man who was never a follower of the American law
I remember the day when he felt the steel of a shotgun, then
    reached for a saw
Like the Lady Liberty, he could hold the heat with one hand
And when it came to shell selection, buck shot, two pumps,
    two he would land
50 grain each, the body had more holes that a brillo pad
no puddle, it was a lake of blood where the body used to stand
I know what you're thinking, it's twisted to describe it like that
You would understand if you had a bug enough ruler to
    measure the hate he had
The cops, he never stayed to see them, he disappeared like vapor
He missed the 5 o'clock news, and never got to read about it in
    the paper
The onlookers, the families, they were shook like a quarter
Not because of the dead, but because they had a killer as a
    neighbor
See, they looked in the box, and saw a pointless homicide
However, if they checked out of it, they would agree it was well
    bonafide
White running from a dead black man, I see how they could
    mistake this
Assumed it was a hate crime, they were quick to call him a
    racist
Little did they know, he helped the community by ridding
    them of a rapist

See, the night before, that dead man was up in his house
Daddy went to tuck baby in,
Entered her room and froze, couldn't get words out of his
    mouth
By the time he thawed, the man was out of the window and
    running down the street
Daddy promised himself and the family
he would settle business next time they meet
See, he made that promise after the cops left his home
The bullshit they fed him, let him know he was in it alone
His baby was a year shy of hitting her first teen years
How it hurt him so bad to see her shed such pain-stricken tears
That night they held each other and cried themselves to sleep
To pool of hate, shame and blame, you can imagine was deep
The next morning came, and he was quick to grab his gun
He was strictly business; his mind frame didn't hold an ounce
    of fun
He hopped in his truck, and drove for a long time
Couldn't find his destination, should have taken it as a sign

Well, he ate lunch, hit the street, and saw him right away
Pump once, click, he was good, would not dare to shoot a stray
The bad man, yes, he quickly hit the ground
Then Daddy walked over to him, said "Remember this face"
Then lit up the pound
The onlookers, yes, they were quick to dial
Staying to get cuffed, that was never his style

I remember seeing on the news, police ripping through hotels
Then hearing they found his room,
then it occurred to ne, Daddy left with three shells
I recall him saying he would go out with a bang, before he sat
     in prison
His intentions were good, but he held the wrong vision
His wife never had the money to get his baby help
Her teens years she medicated with dope, and was never again
     herself
His baby was swallowed by the streets, and hasn't been seen in
     years
As a big brother and son, I wish I'd spoke up on the night of
     shed tears

Death

Death brings us to a better place
I doubt it
A simple message with no explanation
I found it
Spewing out of preachers' mouths
It's becoming a trend over and over again
Constantly being said
Is that why we're killing the living
To help the others
Do we really know
Death is better than breathing
Dead
Or is it because in the afterlife
There is no such thing as deceiving
Death
What kind of truth-stretching crazy out of control lie is that
Not even a good conversation piece
A wasted time to chit chat
Eating applesauce and vodka
To trips into space
A suicidal group

Wonder if they made it to their place
Wonderful world
With pots of gold at the end of the rainbow
What a great place if you decide to say yes
I can tell you one thing
I want to be leaving soon
So trips to never or wonderland
Or to the moon
Yeah, I'll sit here and watch my life deteriorate
But I guess that's all part of the Big Man's fate
And so is the famous phrase
Death

Driving This Journey Forward

Some people dream all day
Me, I dream all day
While standing on Earth
I'm gonna make the best out of my stay
See, I sit in class
Future daydreaming a lot
Trying to think of the forward march
With the talents I got
Right now my days seem like nightmares
And I keep falling
Hands tied, mouth sealed,
So no one can hear me calling
Which path to take
Which way to turn
I have no clue
See, I'm driving this journey forward
But only at my rear view
Future I'm liking

Yet still stuck in my past
People say, "You'll get through it"
But, seriously, how long will this last?
See, God made me strong
But there's only so much a person can take
Everyone knows it was 1 piece of hay
That made the camel's back break
I wish I knew what piece of hay
Will make be crumble
I know I've tripped a lot in my life
But when will I stumble?